Introdu

The present East Lancashire Railway was born from humble beginnings, going as far back as 1966 when steam was still operating on the British Railways mainline. Nowadays, it is one of the premier standard-gauge, preserved railways in the United Kingdom.

The railway has its beginnings with the formation of the Helmshore and District Railway Preservation Society in 1966. It was established with the hope of reopening the Stubbins Junction (Ramsbottom) to Accrington line, which was closed the same year as part of the infamous Beeching cuts. This was part of the Manchester Victoria via Bury to Bacup and Accrington lines, which were opened by the East Lancashire Railway in 1844 and then amalgamated with the Lancashire & Yorkshire Railway (LYR) in 1859. In 1922, the LYR was merged with the London & North Western Railway, but this was short-lived as a year later it became part of one of the 'Big Four' railway companies, namely the London & Midland Scottish Railway, until nationalisation in 1948 when it became British Railways.

Although the Stubbins Junction to Accrington line was closed in 1966, the line between Bury and Rawtenstall remained opened for passenger trains until June 1972 and finally closed in 1980 after the cessation of the coal trains to Rawtenstall. In 1966, the Helmshore and District Railway Preservation Society was formed, as mentioned above, but little progress had been made in reopening the Stubbins Junction to Accrington line and the society ultimately folded; however, from the ashes the East Lancashire Railway Preservation Society (ELRPS) was formed. Their objective was to preserve and operate a smaller section of the line under the banner of the East Lancashire Light Railway (ELLR), but only as far as Haslingden, rather than to Accrington. By 1972, however, this objective was abandoned due to lack of support by the local authorities along with the condition of the track and infrastructure.

But all was not lost, as when the Bury to Rawtenstall line stopped carrying passengers in 1972 it was seen by ELRPS and ELLR as an opportunity to preserve this line instead. By good fortune, Castlecroft Goods Yard and the former goods shed became available and were leased from Bury Council, and the group's railway assets were transferred from Helmshore. On 26 August 1972, under the name of Bury Transport Museum, the location was opened to the public for the first time. By doing this, which included operating brake van rides in Castlecroft Goods Yard, it enabled the combined two groups to raise funds in order to reopen the Bury to Rawtenstall line in the future.

The cessation of the twice-weekly coal trains in 1980 led to the Greater Manchester County Council and Rossendale Borough Council discussing the purchase of the line and infrastructure with British Rail, which eventually proved successful. In November 1984, the East Lancashire Railway Trust (ELRT) was formed as a partnership between the two authorities and the East Lancashire Light Railway to take forward the reopening of the line to trains once again. With the additional role of the ELPS, who provided a volunteer workforce among other things, the success of the partnership came to fruition when, on 25 July 1987, the section of line from Bury to Ramsbottom (a total of 4 miles) was reopened. The first passenger train was hauled by two industrial steam locomotives – former Manchester Ship Canal 0-6-0T No. 32 *Gothenburg* and RSH 0-6-0T ELR No. 1 – and thereafter continued to operate the passenger trains for the remainder of year.

Over the next four years, the railway concentrated on improving existing facilities as well as completing major works on the line between Ramsbottom and Rawtenstall. On 27 April 1991, this section of line was finally opened to traffic, although the station building at Rawtenstall was not completed until the following year. At that time the railway was slowly gaining a good reputation and passenger numbers were steadily increasing – no surprise given the line was in the Greater Manchester conurbation, giving access to over 4 million people. Although the railway was using industrial locomotives to haul passenger trains, it was not long before the first ex-British Railways locomotives arrived, including Derek Foster's LMS 0-6-0T Jinty No. 7298 in 1988 and BR 2-6-0 Standard 4 No. 76079 in 1989. Thereafter the railway began to use ex-British Railway locomotives only for passenger trains, although the odd ex-industrial locomotive still made an occasional appearance.

Although the railway was primarily steam operated in the early years, it acknowledged early on that ex-British Rail diesels could assist operationally and also offer opportunities by holding regular gala events to the growing diesel enthusiast fraternity, which proved very popular. During the 1990s, the railway was gaining an excellent reputation and, in consequence, it received the visit of many ex-British Railway steam locomotives including LNER Class A3 No. 4472 *Flying Scotsman*, BR Class A4 No. 60007 *Sir Nigel Gresley*, BR Coronation Class No. 46229 *Duchess of Hamilton*, BR Standard 8P No. 71000 *Duke of Gloucester*, as well as other big and small locomotives, along with home-based ex-LMS 2-6-0 Crab No. 42765. Add to that the many ex-British Rail diesel locomotives that appeared, including Deltics, Peaks, Fifties and Whistlers, and the East Lancashire Railway made a railway for all occasions and interests.

I first visited the railway in 1988 with the arrival of Jinty No. 7298, and continued to visit until 2001 when other interests took over. In that time (along with many other steam photographers) I realised that, with the railway being on a north to south axis and with the sun going from east to west, there was huge potential in creating spectacular steam images. Although I accept some steam images in this book may be not to everyone's taste, they have been purely taken from a photography point of view with emphasis on lighting and atmospheric conditions. I have attempted to balance it with conventional images throughout the book too and hopefully this represents a true reflection of the railway, including various locations and locomotives during the 1990s.

Finally, I would like to express my personal thanks to Brian Dobbs, Fred Kerr and Kevin Truby, who provided additional images for this book. Their time and patience was very much appreciated. I would also like to express my gratitude to the many people I encountered on visits to the railway, including the drivers, firemen, guards, station staff and numerous volunteers who worked behind the scenes to produce goods; their time and efforts should not be underestimated, as without them there would be no railway. Thank you again and hopefully you will enjoy the contents of this book.

Doug Birmingham
Liverpool

A view of the disused Bury Bolton Street station taken on 29 August 1983. The station was closed on 14 March 1980 after the withdrawal of train service from Manchester Victoria and only come back into use in 1986 when the East Lancashire Railway, with the assistance of the local council, took over the location for the commencement of a train service initially to Ramsbottom, then onwards to Rawtenstall.

When the railway recommenced the train service to Ramsbottom and Rawtenstall in 1987, they used ex-industrial steam locomotives to operate the passenger trains, including Hunslet 0-6-0ST No. 193 *Shropshire*, as seen in this image from 5 May 1991. Looking on are the author's three children as they watch the train depart Irwell Vale station with the 11.00 Bury to Rawtenstall train.

Although this image was not taken in the 1990s it is worthy of inclusion as the locomotive portrayed is former LMS Jinty 0-6-0T No. 7298 – the first ex-British Railways locomotive to work on the reopened line, staying there until 1990. Seen here is No. 7298, owned at the time by Derek Foster, on a cold misty Sunday crossing Brooksbottom Viaduct and approaching the entrance to Nuttall Tunnel with 12.00 Bury to Ramsbottom Santa Special. (27 November 1988)

Another locomotive owned by Derek Foster at the time was ex-British Railways Standard Class 4MT locomotive, No. 76079, which arrived at the railway earlier in the year and became a popular locomotive on the line. By coincidence both Nos 7289 and 76079 were allocated to the same British Railways steam shed prior to withdrawal in the mid-1960s – St Helens Sutton Oak (8G). The locomotive is seen here working hard with six matching maroon coaches through Burrs Cutting on the 13.00 Bury to Ramsbottom train. (4 November 1990)

Seen here in excellent lighting conditions and working across Brooksbottom Viaduct is another Standard 4MT Class locomotive. This time it is No. 75078 visiting from the Keighley & Worth Valley Railway in tandem with No. 76079 on the 14.00 Bury to Ramsbottom train. As you can see, the viaduct was rather close to the homes of the local residents and no doubt they felt, let alone heard, the power of locomotives working past. (4 November 1990)

One hour later from the previous image and the stunning lighting conditions highlight No. 76079 and its train to good effect. The locomotive had returned to Bury to work the 15.00 train to Ramsbottom. Taken from the overlooking park, presenting a wider view of Brooksbottom Viaduct, it is seen working away from Summerseat. (4 November 1990)

Proving popular with enthusiasts and passengers alike, Derek Foster's two locomotives were working the majority of the weekend trains on the line. With a partial reflection in the river below, No. 76079, with the 14.00 Bury to Rawtenstall train, is gently working across the River Irwell bridge at Fernhill, the latter being the name of the nearby residential area. (12 May 1991)

Compared with the previous image, this shows the train at track level as it crosses the River Irwell bridge. Looking out of the cab-side window is Derek Foster who is driving his locomotive, No. 76079, with its six coaches as it crosses the River Irwell bridge at Fernhill with the 16.00 Bury to Rawtenstall train. (12 May 1991)

Visiting the railway for the first time was ex-LNER Class N7 0-6-2T No. 69621, which was on loan from the East Anglia Railway Museum. It is seen crossing Brooksbottom Viaduct – this time from road level – with the 17.00 Bury to Rawtenstall train on 12 May 1991. No. 69621 was the final locomotive built at Stratford Works, London, in 1924. It was part of a batch of twenty-two locomotives and primarily worked on the Metropolitan lines in London before withdrawal by British Railway in September 1962.

What may have been the first time, even during British Railways steam days, is the unusual appearance of a former BR Western locomotive Manor Class 4-6-0, No. 7828 *Odney Manor*, arriving at the surroundings of Ramsbottom station in the heart of Lancashire. The locomotive was on the 10.00 Bury to Rawtenstall train. It had previously arrived from the Llangollen Railway and was set about to work the line's passenger services almost immediately. (1 September 1991)

This image shows the station's water tank, signals and signal box to advantage, along with the gates to Bridge Street crossing. No. 7828 *Odney Manor* waits to depart with its train for Rawtenstall on 1 September 1991. The latter station and section of line opened on 27 April 1991 with a special train hauled by 0-6-0Ts No. 32 *Gothenburg* and ELR 'No 1'. Previously these same two locomotives hauled the line's reopening special from Bury to Ramsbottom on 25 July 1987.

On a late summer morning, shortly after departing Irwell Vale station on the reopened Ramsbottom to Rawtenstall section of line, Standard 4MT No. 76079 approaches Blackburn Road (B6527) bridge at Ewood Bridge with the 10.00 Bury to Rawtenstall train. In the background is the peak of Scholes Height, which is part of Holcombe Moor. (15 September 1991)

With the rich, deep colours of autumn showing to advantage, ex-BR Southern West Country Class, No. 34072 *257 Squadron* crosses the River Irwell, Fernhill, with the 14.00 Bury to Rawtenstall train. Owned by the Southern Locomotives Ltd, the West Country locomotive had operated on the mainline in 1990, but it had arrived from the North Yorkshire Moors Railway in October and stayed at the ELR for almost twelve months before moving to the Swanage Railway. (9 November 1991)

In surreal lighting conditions, which add to the atmospheric conditions, No. 34072 *257 Squadron* powers its nine-coach train past the foot crossing at Burrs with the 11.00 Bury to Rawtenstall Santa Special on 7 December 1991. No. 34072 was built at Brighton in April 1948 and operated on the Southern region before being withdrawn in late 1964. She was then towed to Woodham Bros scrapyard, Barry, in February 1965 and it was another nineteen years before it got rescued and restoration began.

An image that was previously published on the back cover of the March 1992 edition of *Railway Magazine*, the author makes no apologies for another airing and thought it worthy of inclusion in this book. On a cold winter's morning, the sun just about rising above the horizon, BR Standard 4MT No. 76079 makes a spirited run past with its goods train passing Burrs foot crossing. It is not always possible to record a train so early in a day, so the solution by a group of photographers was to hire the train and line for the day – hence this image. (10 January 1992)

Taken the same morning as the previous image, BR Standard 4MT No. 76079, with its eleven-wagon goods train, works hard across Brooksbottom Viaduct as it approaches the entrance to Nuttall Tunnel on 10 January 1992. This vantage point clearly shows the width of the viaduct to indicate it once accommodated two tracks before it was lifted by British Rail during the 1970s.

The third and final image taken from 10 January 1992, and now taking advantage of the afternoon sunset, is of No. 76079 and its goods train approaching Horncliffe Crossing, just south of Townsend Fold on the Ramsbottom to Rawtenstall section of line. The lighting conditions on this day was a dream for photographers during the 7 hours of daylight that was available – ideal to record steam at work.

To add variety for the visiting enthusiast, the ELR always provided interesting locomotive combinations during Gala events and this was no exception. In this instance, a combination that was once a common sight on the Somerset & Dorset line in British Railways days. Ex-Southern West Country No. 34072 *257 Squadron* leads Standard 4MT No. 76079 during a Winter Steam Gala weekend event with the 13.00 Bury to Rawtenstall train as it approaches Burrs Cutting. (26 January 1992)

Again during the Winter Steam Gala weekend, the ELR provided an unusual combination of BR Western Manor and BR Southern West Country locomotives. Seen here is No. 34072 *257 Squadron* and No. 7828 *Odney Manor* as they provide a spectacular display powering their short five-coach train as they pass Burrs foot crossing with the 11.00 Bury to Rawtenstall train. (26 January 1992)

Looking east and taken from the top of Holcombe Hill, which overlooks the line between Bury and Ramsbottom, No. 7828 *Odney Manor* leads No. 34072 *257 Squadron* on the 14.00 Bury to Rawtenstall train as it crosses Brooksbottom Viaduct in the village of Summerseat. Towards the top of the image you are able to follow the line of the M66 and beyond, in the haze, looking east towards the Pennine Hills. (26 January 1992)

An interesting record shot of Standard 4MT No. 76079 posing with former LMS Cravens 50T Steam Crane with support coach and brake van at Fernhill (sometimes known as Little Burrs Cutting) on 20 March 1992. The crane, seen here in steam, was built by Cravens Brothers in 1931 (works No. 126836) for the London Midland & Scottish Railway, numbered 'MP8' and initially had a 36-tonne capacity before it was upgraded to 50 tonnes.

The first of two images taken on a cool summer day. Midland Fowler 4f No. 4422, visiting from the North Staffordshire Railway (now the Churnet Valley Railway) for a few months, ploughs through Burrs Cutting with four carmine and cream coaches in tow on the 13.00 Bury to Rawtenstall train. Traditionally, most steam photographers tend to hide during the summer, as hot summer temperatures tend not to be ideal for good steam photography, but today was an exception. (12 July 1992)

The unpredictable changes of the weather in our country sometimes produces unexpected cool conditions in the height of the summer, and this day was no exception. The second image from 12 July 1992, an hour after the previous image, and West Country Class locomotive No. 34072 *257 Squadron* and its five maroon coaches gently ambles through Burrs Cutting on the 14.00 Bury to Rawtenstall train just as the sun makes a timely appearance.

On a clear, late, summer's afternoon, Fowler 4f No. 4422 works across Brooksbottom Viaduct with the 17.00 Bury to Rawtenstall train. Around the viaduct is the village of Summerseat and seen at the rear of the train is old goods warehouse, which was sold by the East Lancashire Railway and subsequently converted into apartments. (12 July 1992)

Approaching New Hall Hey Road bridge, Fowler 4f No. 4422 is near the end of its journey with the 17.00 Bury to Rawtenstall train on 12 July 1992. At the rear of the train is Townsend Fold signal box and road crossing, and in the distance is Peel Tower, which is at the top of Holcombe Hill. The tower is named after Sir Robert Peel, who was born in Bury and became prime minister in the 1830s.

Passing the location known as the Drum Works, with the bridge leading to Chamberhall Street, Bury, in the background, Fowler 4f No. 4422 heads to Ramsbottom on the 15.00 Bury to Rawtenstall train. The 4f was built at the LMS Derby Works in 1927 and spent its life initially in the Midlands, then transferred to South West England until withdrawal in 1965 when it was taken to Woodham Brothers scrapyard and finally rescued in 1977 for restoration. (15 September 1992)

A smoke display for the photographer's gallery at Fernhill. It was just as well the wind was blowing to the right otherwise there may have been some unhappy residents who could have had their washing hanging out to dry. Manor Class No. 7828 *Odney Manor*, complete with Cambrian Coast Express headboard, works past with the 17.00 Bury to Rawtenstall train. (27 September 1992)

Three locomotives that all arrived at the railway during late autumn in 1992, and the opportunity was taken to record them together under floodlights outside Castlecroft Shed. From left to right: GWR 4-6-0 Castle Class No. 5029 *Nunney Castle* and GWR 2-8-0T No. 5224 (arguably the most famous locomotive in the world) LNER 4-6-2 Class A3 No. 4472 *Flying Scotsman*, which was commencing a three-month visit to the railway. (Courtesy of Brian Dobbs)

Having arrived from Didcot Railway Centre, former Great Western locomotive 4-6-0 Castle Class No. 5029 *Nunney Castle* was quickly put into use over the Christmas period and certainly proved popular, not just with the passengers but the photographers too for producing extraordinary steam effects. The Castle Class locomotive is earning its keep here hauling a nine-coach Santa Special through Fernhill (Little Burrs Cutting) with the 12.15 Bury to Rawtenstall train on 13 December 1992.

Appearing as long-lost classmate, No. 44311 Fowler 4f No. 4422 simmers gently with its goods train at Bury Bolton Street station on 3 December 1992. The reason for appearing as No. 44311 was because it was a local locomotive in British Railways steam days, especially during the 1950s where it was based at 26A Newton Heath Shed, Manchester. The original No. 44311 survived until July 1966 and was ultimately scrapped at Drapers in Hull.

On a cold frosty morning, almost the shortest day of the year, the sun barely risen, No. 7828 *Odney Manor* makes a spectacular exhaust with its short empty coach train to Ramsbottom. It was common practice during the Christmas period to operate a steam-hauled shuttle train between Ramsbottom and Rawtenstall while the main Santa trains terminated at Ramsbottom for operational reasons. To facilitate this the railway always operated an empty train prior to the commencement of the day's Santa timetable, which was a bonus for the photographers. (20 December 1992)

Approaching Blackburn Road bridge (Ewood Bridge), former Great Western 2-8-0T No. 5224 works the 10.15 Ramsbottom to Rawtenstall shuttle on 20 December 1992. No. 5224 had arrived from the Great Central Railway in early November and stayed until spring 1993. The locomotive, designed by G. J. Churchward, was built at Swindon in 1924 and spent most of its life in South Wales until it was withdrawn by British Railways in April 1963.

Having just departed from Summerseat station, GWR No. 5029 *Nunney Castle* works hard away with its nine-coach train across Brooksbottom Viaduct with the 11.00 Bury to Ramsbottom Santa Special. No. 5029 *Nunney Castle* was designed by C. B. Collett and built at Swindon Works in 1934 before being withdrawn by British Railways at the end of 1963. (20 December 1992)

On a very cold frosty morning with steam enveloping the entire train, GWR 2-8-0T No. 5224 leads LMS 4f No. 4422 away from the last departure stop at Summerseat station and is now approaching Brooksbottom Viaduct with the 10.00 Bury to Rawtenstall train. At Ramsbottom No. 5224 will be detached from the train, with the 4f proceeding forward to Rawtenstall. (29 December 1992)

With the axis of the railway line generally being of a north–south direction, it does lend itself especially well during the winter for silhouette shots against the setting sunset. The next two images highlight this potential at the River Irwell bridge, Fernhill, where there is only an hour between each image. Both images were taken on 20 December 1992.

Top image: With the sun shining 2-8-0T No. 5224 crosses the bridge with the 14.45 Bury to Ramsbottom Santa Special. *Bottom image*: The sun has now set beyond the houses in the background, leaving a golden glow in the sky. No. 5029 *Nunney Castle* rushes past with the 16.00 Bury to Ramsbottom Santa Special.

Another two images of Fowler 4f No. 4422, this time in the disguise of long-lost classmate No. 44311. Both images were taken on 29 December 1992.

Top image: With waiting passengers on the platform, No. 44311 arrives at Summerseat station with the 12.00 Bury to Rawtenstall train. The next stop would be Ramsbottom station. *Bottom image*: With the winter sun now slowly setting, light reflects off No. 44311, which is approaching Horncliffe Crossing as it passes the outer home signal for Townsend Fold with the 14.00 Bury to Rawtenstall train.

Having photographed the 4f at Ramsbottom station, a quick dash in the car to Blackburn Road bridge (Ewood Bridge) gave the opportunity to record a second image of the train. Remaining in its disguise of No. 44311, Fowler 4f No. 4422 with four carmine and cream coaches in tow is seen approaching the bridge. (29 December 1992)

With the railway line only 8 miles in length, it is inevitable that some locations become more popular more than others, and the River Irwell Bridge at Fernhill is one of them. In this instance, working the 16.00 Bury to Rawtenstall train as it crosses the bridge, the outline of 4f No. 4422 against the setting sun is very distinct, showing the gap between the boiler and the frames as well as the coal rails on the tender. (17 January 1993)

Two images featuring GWR 2-8-0T No. 5224 on its seven-coach train. Both were taken on the glorious sunny day of 29 December 1992 – just one of those days where things could (unusually) not go wrong.

Top image: No. 5224 storms out of Nuttall Tunnel and passes the distant signal for Ramsbottom station with the 13.00 Bury to Rawtenstall train. *Bottom image*: Having just departed from Irwell Vale station, No. 5224 works up the straight valley of trees towards Ewood Bridge with the 11.00 Bury to Rawtenstall train.

Framed between the home signals at the south end of Ramsbottom station, Great Western locomotives 2-8-0T No. 5224 leading 4-6-0 No. 5029 *Nunney Castle* arrive for the midway stop on the line with the 10.00 Bury to Rawtenstall train during the Winter Steam Gala weekend on 31 January 1993.

In soft afternoon winter sun, Fowler 4f No. 4422 is on the approach to Horncliffe Crossing, near Townsend Fold, with the 15.00 Bury to Rawtenstall train on 31 January 1993. No. 4422's restoration from scrapyard condition took fifteen years, and it became the first resident locomotive to work on the North Staffordshire Railway (now Churnet Valley Railway) in 1992.

Taken from the road embankment of the A56 at Ewood Bridge, Great Western 4-6-0 No. 5029 *Nunney Castle* approaches the photographer with the 15.00 Bury to Rawtenstall train on 21 February 1993. In the background is Blackburn Road bridge, and the distant signal for Townsend Fold. No. 5029 was purchased from Woodham Bros of Barry in 1976 – it became the last locomotive to leave that location by rail. It was restored at the Didcot Railway Centre and finally entered service in 1990.

Coming towards the end of her loan period at the railway, LNER A3 No. 4472 *Flying Scotsman* is seen crossing the River Irwell between Irwell Vale and Ewood Bridge with the 12.00 Bury to Rawtenstall train on 21 February 1993. All was not well with *Flying Scotsman*, however, as a couple of weeks later No. 4472 was declared a failure and repairs were needed before she could return to steam some months later. (Courtesy of Kevin Truby)

The year 1993 saw the arrival of the first Black Five to the railway in the form of Paddy Smith's mainline-certified locomotive No. 5407. Ever since then, Black Fives have always featured on the railway – probably more so than any other locomotive class. Unusual at the time, No. 5407 arrived with the locomotive facing south, therefore providing an opportunity to photograph at untried locations. In this view No. 5407 departs from Irwell Vale station with the 12.00 Rawtenstall to Bury train. (21 March 1993)

Another opportunity was taken with the visiting Fowler 4f No. 4422 to change her identity for a private charter, this time in the form of No. 44525, an ex-Llandudno Junction (6G) locomotive. The real No. 44525 was the last of her class to work for British Railways before being withdrawn from Crewe Works in 1966. In this view, the 4f departed from Nuttall Tunnel with a short goods train, mainly consisting of four-wheel tanks. (13 April 1993)

Following on from the above image, No. 44525 has now arrived at Ramsbottom station to take on water as well as having a crew break before the train proceeds to Rawtenstall. The view gives a general ambience of a BR London Midland town station in the 1950s, complete with signal box and road crossing, along with the four-wheel 12T box van behind the locomotive – commonplace in those days. (13 April 1993)

Visiting from the Didcot Railway Centre as part of the railway's Festival of Steam event, Hawksworth Modified Hall Class locomotive No. 6998 *Burton Agnes Hall*, on an afternoon Bury to Rawtenstall train, works over Brooksbottom Viaduct with the village of Summerseat overseeing the scene. Although No. 6998 is a Great Western-designed locomotive, she was built by British Railways in 1949 at Swindon Works, and withdrawn in early 1966 and rescued for preservation by the Great Western Society shortly afterwards. (August 1993)

With 2-10-0 9f No. 92203 and 4MT 2-6-0 No. 76079 providing the backdrop in Buckley Wells yard, five gentlemen posed for the camera in August 1993. Left to right: Chris Beet, who maintained Ivatt 2-6-0 No. 46441; the late Paddy Smith, owner of Black Five, No. 5407; Brian Topping, driver at the ELR; and two more true gentlemen, the late David Shepherd, owner of 9f No. 92203, and Derek Foster, owner of 4MT No. 76079. Certainly an image that will never be repeated.

Coasting across Holme Lane Crossing, former Great Western Churchward design 2-8-0, 2800 class, No. 2857 is passing Townsend Fold signal box on the 10.00 Bury to Rawtenstall train on 8 August 1993. In plain black BR livery, No. 2857 had arrived at the railway as part of the Festival of Steam event from the Severn Valley Railway. No. 2857 was built in 1918 at Swindon Works and had a long working life before being withdrawn by British Railways in April 1963.

Another former GWR locomotive had also arrived in time for the Festival of Steam event: No. 3822, a modified Collet 2-8-0 design visiting from the Didcot Railway Centre. Approaching the little cutting at Fernhill, No. 3822 takes its seven coaches in its stride on the 12.00 Bury to Rawtenstall train on 14 August 1993. (Courtesy of Kevin Truby)

Owned by the famous wildlife artist David Shepherd is former British Railways Standard Class 9f 2-10-0 No. 92203 *Black Prince*, seen here standing outside Buckley Wells shed under the floodlights with a breakdown train. The locomotive was another visitor to the railway as part of their Festival of Steam event to mark the 25th anniversary of the end of steam on British Railways in 1968. As part of the festival the railway arranged an evening/night shoot with various locomotives under the floodlights. (20 August 1993)

Another view of No. 92203 *Black Prince*, this time from the rear. The floodlights certainly show off her unique 2-10-0 wheel arrangement, along with the high running plate too. The 9f was built in 1959 at Swindon Works and had only a working life of under nine years before she withdrawn in November 1967. She had been working iron ore trains between Bidston Dock, Birkenhead and Shotton steelworks. The locomotive was then purchased by David Shepherd and moved to the Longmoor Military Railway where she was eventually named *Black Prince*. (20 August 1993)

The lighting effect created by different temperature floodlights in and around Buckley Wells shed produces a surreal rear image of Jubilee Class locomotive No. 45596 *Bahamas*. This locomotive was built by the London Midland & Scottish Railway in 1935, designed by William Stanier and withdrawn by British Railways in July 1966, but not before she received her double chimney in 1961. No. 45596 was purchased by the Stockport (Bahamas) Locomotive Society in 1967 and in 1968 she was based at the Dinting Railway Centre, then Keighley & Worth Valley Railway. (20 August 1993)

Another first-time visitor to the railway was ex-Southern Railways Class S15 4-6-0 No. 30506 from the Mid Hants Railway. It is seen under the floodlights as part of the Festival of Steam event at Buckley Wells on 20 August 1993. The locomotive operated some passenger trains on the railway, including a double-header with another ex-Southern locomotive, No. 35005 *Canadian Pacific*. No. 30506 was built at Eastleigh Works in 1920 and remained in service under 1964 when she was withdrawn by British Railways and taken to Woodham Bros, Barry for scrapping. However, she was rescued by Urie Locomotive Society and eventually restored to working order in 1987.

Another image taken at Buckley Wells shed on the evening of 27 August 1993. Perhaps the only occasion these three locomotives have all been together. From left to right: ex-Somerset & Dorset 7f 2-8-0 locomotive No. 53809, ex-British Railways double-chimney Jubilee Class locomotive, No. 45596 *Bahamas* and finally another Jubilee – a single chimney example in ex-LMS livery, No. 5593 *Kolaphur*.

Showing its unique disc wheels to advantage, ex-Southern Railways 4-6-2 Merchant Navy Class No. 35005 *Canadian Pacific* simmers in Buckley Wells shed yard on the second of the Festival of Steam evening photo shoots on 27 August 1993. No. 35005 was built in 1941 as a mixed-traffic locomotive and was initially made with air smooth casing. It was rebuilt in it's current form in 1959 by British Railways and subsequently withdrawn in late 1965. No. 35005 was purchased privately in 1973 from Woodham Bros, where it was eventually returned to steam in 1990.

As part of the Festival of Steam event the railway hired a number of visiting locomotives. They were mostly working examples, but they also took the opportunity to bring in, as a static exhibit, ex-LMS Coronation Class No. 6233 *Duchess of Sutherland* from the Bressingham Railway Museum. No. 6233 was initially acquired by Butlins from British Railways in 1964 and put on display at their Head of Ayr holiday camp before being purchased by Bressingham. She is seen here on display in Buckley Wells shed in her LMS livery and without her smoke deflectors. (20 August 1993)

Visiting from the Keighley & Worth Valley Railway, again as part of the Festival of Steam event, was BR 2-8-0 8f No. 48431. It is seen in soft light approaching Blackburn Road bridge with the 09.00 Bury to Rawtenstall train on 28 August 1993. No. 48431 was built at Swindon Works in 1944 and withdrawn in 1964, then despatched to Woodham Bros, Barry, before being rescued for preservation in 1972 where she is the only surviving Swindon-built 8f locomotive. (Courtesy of Kevin Truby)

Using a short telephoto lens and approaching New Hall Hey Road bridge, Jubilee Class No. 45596 *Bahamas*, with its six maroon coaches, works away from Townsend Fold signal box. The locomotive is now on the final approach to Rawtenstall station with the ex-10.00 departure from Bury Bolton Street station. (12 September 1993)

Taken on 12 September 1993, former Somerset & Dorset Joint Railway 7f 2-8-0 No. 53809, with a matching rake of carmine and cream coaches, approaches Blackburn Road bridge (Ewood Bridge) on the 11.00 Bury to Rawtenstall train. No. 53809 was part of a batch of eleven locomotives designed by Henry Fowler and was built as No. 89 in 1925 at the Robert Stephenson & Co. works in Darlington. It was finally withdrawn, moved to Woodham Bros of Barry in 1964 and stayed there until 1975 when it was privately purchased.

Not all is what it seems in this image. What appears to be BR Coronation Class 4-6-2 locomotive No. 46246 *City of Manchester* with 'The Caledonian' headboard at Bury Bolton Street station is in fact No. 46233 *Duchess of Sutherland*, appearing as one of her former classmates. The real No. 46246 was withdrawn and scrapped in 1963 at Crewe Works. (14 September 1993)

The opportunity was taken by the author to change the appearance of No. 6233 to another classmate, namely No. 46247 *City of Liverpool*. This rear view shows the yellow stripe on the cab, which represents the locomotive was not allowed to work under the electric wires during the early 1960s. While in reality No. 46247 never appeared with the stripe, No. 46246 did. Visually there are minor differences between the locomotives, as No. 6246 and No. 46247 were originally built as streamlined locomotives, unlike No, 46233, which was built in conventional form in 1938. (14 September 1993)

Passing Horncliffe Crossing and the distant signal for Townsend Fold, Black Five No. 5407 gently heads to its next stop at Irwell Vale with the 13.00 Rawtenstall to Bury train on 12 September 1993. No. 5407 was built at the Armstrong Whitworth works, Newcastle upon Tyne, in 1937 for the LMS and was one of the final locomotives to be withdrawn by British Railways on 4 August 1968. It was then privately purchased, based at Steamtown, Carnforth, before being sold to Paddy Smith in 1974.

With Irwell Vale station in the background, Black Five No. 5407 is still facing the south works on the 12.00 Rawtenstall to Bury train. Next stop, Ramsbottom station. Initially, the locomotive was only visiting the railway for a few months, but agreement was reached between Paddy Smith and railway for the locomotive to be permanently based at the railway while between mainline operations. In 1997, the locomotive was sold to resident mechanical engineer Ian Riley, who has owned the locomotive ever since. (27 November 1993)

Framed by a convenient tree approaching Touch Hill Cutting and in late afternoon autumn sunshine, Midland Fowler 7f No. 53809 approaches the photographer with a nice trailing steam exhaust and the 15.00 Bury to Rawtenstall train. (21 November 1993)

Next stop, Bury Bolton Street station, silhouetted by the setting sun. Black Five No. 5407, with assistance from the footplate crew, works across the River Irwell bridge at Fernhill with the 16.00 ex-Rawtenstall train. Under normal operating conditions most southbound steam trains were coasting on this location, therefore you had to prearrange for some exhaust and kindly ask the driver to open up just before the location. Most times it worked, but occasionally the driver unintentionally forgot. (21 November 1993)

With the visit of 7f No. 53809 the opportunity was taken by a local photographer to organise a private photographic charter, matching the locomotive with a goods train consisting of six 12t box vans and two open wagons. With the sun timely breaking through and the steam exhaust highlighting the train to good effect, No. 53809 approaches the gallery at Burrs on 12 December 1993.

Taken on the same day as the previous image and framed by a convenient tree, No. 53809 and its goods train passes the distant signal for Ramsbottom station near Nuttall Park, having just left the same named tunnel a few seconds earlier. The 7f was a popular locomotive during its stay, but returned to its home base at the Midland Railway, Butterley, in early 1994. (12 December 1993)

Having visited the railway a year earlier, former Great Western 2-8-0T No. 5224 returned for another short stay in and around the Christmas period in 1993. On a cold morning and with a light covering of snow on the hills, the driver of No. 5224 keeps the steam on as she slows down for the stop at Irwell Vale station with the 10.00 Bury to Rawtenstall train. (26 December 1993)

An hour after the previous image of No. 5224 and the light covering of snow had melted away when Manor Class locomotive No. 7828 *Odney Manor* departed from Irwell Vale station with the 11.00 Bury to Rawtenstall train. Irwell Vale became a popular location with photographers, not just for the photographic possibilities but also due to the local church community hall. On most Sundays they had a tea room providing hot drinks and food, which as you can imagine was well received, especially on cold days during the winter. (26 December 1993)

Working hard and approaching Stubbins, just north of Ramsbottom, is No. 7828 *Odney Manor* on the 13.00 Bury to Rawtenstall train. In the background are remnants of the local Victorian cotton industry. The two tall chimneys were once a feature in most Lancashire towns, but nowadays are not so commonplace as, in the name of progress and a changing world, cotton is now mainly produced outside the United Kingdom. (26 December 1993)

One of the most anticipated events in steam preservation was the return to steam of a L&YR Hughes 2-6-0 Mogul locomotive – the last occasion was in 1967. The railway owned one of three surviving locomotives of the class – No 42765 – and after a fairly lengthy restoration finally returned it to steam in late 1993. Seen here on one of its early workings is No. 42765, making light work of its train as it crosses the embankment at Burrs with the 13.00 Bury to Rawtenstall train on 23 January 1994.

Having just exited Nuttall Tunnel and passing the distant signal for Ramsbottom station, No. 7828 Odney Manor is just about to shut off steam and commence slowdown in order to stop at the station before proceeding to Irwell Vale on the 13.00 Bury to Rawtenstall train. (30 January 1994)

With the return to steam of 2-6-0 Mogul No. 42765 it was not long before a private charter was arranged, with the locomotive hauling what may have been a typical goods train of the early 1960s. On what turned out to be an excellent day weather wise, the light reflects nicely off the locomotive hauling its twelve-vehicle train as it approaches Touch Hill Cutting at Burrs. This particular class of locomotive received the nickname of 'Crab' due to the resemblance to a crab's pincers of the outside cylinders and valve motion. (28 January 1994)

Later in the afternoon than the image above, and looking along the River Irwell, No. 42765 crosses Brooksbottom Viaduct at Summerseat with its goods train as it approaches Nuttall Tunnel on 28 January 1994. No. 42765 was designed by George Hughes, the Chief Mechanical Engineer of the London Midland & Scottish Railway, and was built at Crewe in 1927 as No. 13065. It was finally withdrawn from British Railways service in December 1966 and taken to Woodham Bros scrapyard in Barry, remaining there until purchase in 1978.

On a clear summer's day and with Peel Tower in the distant background, former LNER A4 4-6-2 Class No. 4498 *Sir Nigel Gresley* passes Townsend Fold signal box on the final few hundred yards to its destination of Rawtenstall station with the 17.00 ex-Bury train. *Sir Nigel Gresley* is seen in her garter blue livery complete with alloy numbers on her cab-side, as well as alloy letters on the tender too. The added touch of 'The Flying Scotsman' headboard provides a reminder of the express service that operated between Kings Cross, London, to Edinburgh in the 1930s. (24 July 1994)

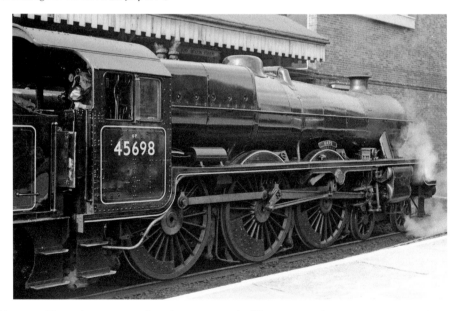

Taken on 25 September 1994, not all is what it seems to be. This appears to be British Railways Jubilee 4-6-0 Class locomotive No. 45698 *Mars* complete in lined-out black livery and Fowler tender at Bury Bolton Street station; however, it is actually LMS Jubilee No. 5593 *Kolaphur* in disguise as one of her long-lost classmates. The real No. 45698 *Mars* was built in 1936 at Crewe Works and was long time resident of Bank Hall (27A) MPD, Liverpool, before being withdrawn by British Railways in October 1965.

With the visit of Jubilee No. 5593 *Kolaphur*, and with the grateful assistance of Birmingham Railway Museum, the ELR and well-known photographer Geoff Silcock, the opportunity was taken to replicate the appearance of the first of the Jubilee Class, No. 5552 *Silver Jubilee*, as she first appeared in 1935. She is seen complete with silver alloy trimmings including raised cab numbers, boiler and cab window bands and around-the-front cylinder among other items. Seen here at Buckley Wells shed accompanied by 8f No. 8431 in September 1994. (Courtesy of Brian Dobbs)

Jubilee No. 5593 *Kolaphur*'s third and final disguise during September 1994 was the reappearance of a local Newton Heath (26A) MPD example: No. 45700 *Amethyst* matched up with Fowler tender from resident Crab No. 42765 to give its authentic appearance as noted during the 1950s. The locomotive is seen here on a private charter hauling eight coaches through Touch Hill Cutting, Burrs, on 22 September 1994.

Taken the same day as the previous image – 22 September 1994 – in late afternoon sun, No. 45700 *Amethyst* and train crosses Brooksbottom Viaduct on the approach to Nuttall Tunnel. The real No. 45700 was built by the LMS in April 1936 as No. 5700 at Crewe Works. It was finally withdrawn by British Railways in mid-1964 when it was allocated to Warrington Dallam (8B) shed and cut up at Crewe Works the same year.

On a crisp sunny morning and taken from the road that leads to the private apartments, a young family takes in the wonderful sight of a steam locomotive: No. 7828 *Odney Manor* crossing Brooksbottom Viaduct with the 10.00 Bury to Rawtenstall train. Next stop, Ramsbottom station. (6 November 1994)

A steady drive after taking the previous image at Brooksbottom Viaduct and the author arrived at Horncliffe Crossing, Townsend Fold, to view Manor Class No. 7828 *Odney Manor* working the final leg of her train to Rawtenstall. In the background you are able to see the vehicles travelling on the A56 dual carriageway, which crosses the line near Ewood Bridge. (6 November 1994)

With the A56 winding its way through the Lancashire countryside, Mogul Crab No. 42765 approaches the distant signal for Townsend Fold with the 11.00 Bury to Rawtenstall train on 6 November 1994. This was taken from the bottom of Dearden Moor.

While the trees around the River Irwell at Fernhill show off their autumn colours, Manor Class No. 7828 *Odney Manor* works across the sunlit bridge with the 14.00 Bury to Rawtenstall train on 6 November 1994.

The golden sunset shows off the unmistakable outline of 4-6-0 Black Five No. 5407 as she heads south at Burrs with the 16.00 Rawtenstall to Bury train on 6 November 1994. Earlier in the day Crab No. 42765 had been working the line's train with No. 7828 *Odney Manor*, but the opportunity was taken to give the Black Five a run out in the late afternoon after recent work was carried out on her to make sure she was fit to run – hence her appearance on this train.

The lights at Buckley Wells shed provide the silhouette head-on effect of a British Railways Standard Class locomotive, this being Class 8 No. 71000 *Duke of Gloucester*. She simmers at the end of the day while she is flanked by two Stanier Class locomotives: Black Five No. 5407 and No. 45996 *Bahamas*. (24 February 1995)

A visitor to the line during the winter from the Birmingham Railway Museum at Tyseley was ex-GWR 0-6-0T *Pannier* No. 7752. She was ideal to haul the line's shorter off-peak service. Passing the distant signal for Ramsbottom station, No. 7752, resplendent in British Railways plain black livery, steams away from Nuttall Tunnel on New Year's Day in 1995 with the 12.00 Bury to Rawtenstall train.

Showing off her new, attractive British Railways lined blue livery to good effect, A4 Class, now No. 60007, *Sir Nigel Gresley* departs Irwell Vale station with the 10.00 Bury to Rawtenstall train during the railway's Winter Steam Gala weekend. (26 February 1995)

Working away from the stop at Ramsbottom station, Class A4 No. 60007 *Sir Nigel Gresley* provides a spirited clean steam exhaust on the 12.00 Bury to Rawtenstall train on 26 February 1995. This photograph was taken on the sidings, which provided additional operational capabilities for the exchange of various locomotives during railway's gala events.

Another visitor to the railway was unique British Railways Standard Class 8, 4-6-2 No. 71000 *Duke of Gloucester*, which was there receiving maintenance work at Ian Riley's workshop pending a return to mainline duties. Seen here at Touch Hill Cutting, Burrs, the *Duke*'s crew provides the photographers with a lovely steam exhaust with a midday Rawtenstall to Bury train on 26 February 1995.

After departing from Ramsbottom station, No. 71000 *Duke of Gloucester* approaches Nuttall Tunnel with the 15.00 Rawtenstall to Bury train on 26 February 1995. The *Duke* was a one-off design by Robert Riddles, CME of British Railways. It was built in 1954 and withdrawn after a short life of eight years in 1962. From there (minus one outside cylinder, which was preserved at the Science Museum) she was taken to Woodham Bros, Barry, to be ultimately scrapped. Fortunately, she was rescued in 1974 and then commenced the long restoration of this unique locomotive to working order, which was no mean feat to say the least.

A lone photographer stands in the field to record the passing of the 14.00 Rawtenstall to Bury train headed by 4-6-0 Black Five No. 5407 and 2-6-0 Ivatt Class 2, No. 46441, which had departed from Ramsbottom station a couple of minutes earlier. Unfortunately for the author both locomotives had shut off steam just before taking the image, but at least it highlights a Sunday football game in the nearby Nuttall Park in Ramsbottom. (26 February 1995)

With Peel Monument on Holcombe Hill in the background, the driver nicely times opening the regulator of 4-6-0 Black Five No. 5407 with 2-6-0 Ivatt Class 2 No. 46441 attached as they approach Burrs Crossing with the 16.00 Rawtenstall to Bury train. (26 February 1995)

On an early spring Sunday morning and nicely framed between two trees, BR Standard 9f No. 92203 *Black Prince* approaches Burrs foot crossing with an empty coach stock working from Bury to Ramsbottom station. (9 April 1995)

On 8 October 1995, a lone waiting passenger watches 4-6-0 Black Five No. 44767 *George Stephenson* arrive at Irwell Vale station with the 11.00 Rawtenstall to Bury train. No. 44767, which was visiting from the North Yorkshire Moors Railway, was unique among the 842-strong class of Black Five locomotives as it was only one built with outside Stephenson link motion (in addition to other experimental features) when she was released into British Railways traffic in 1948. She was withdrawn in 1967 before being purchased for preservation by Ian Storey and returned to working order in 1975.

The author's eldest son watches Black Five No. 5407 quietly pass over the River Irwell bridge and approaching Irwell Vale with the 12.00 Rawtenstall to Bury train on 8 October 1995. Little did we know at the time of the photograph that my son would actually work on this locomotive, being employed by Ian Riley at Buckley Wells. He would eventually become a mainline fireman, where he has had the privilege of firing this locomotive, among many others, on the United Kingdom mainlines.

On what may have been its first public outing, former Lancashire & Yorkshire Railway 0-6-0 Class 27 No. 52322 leads 4-6-0 Black Five No. 45337 on a mid-afternoon Bury to Rawtenstall train as it approaches Burrs foot crossing on 8 October 1995. By coincidence both locomotives had only just been restored back into working order, with No. 45337 working its first trains since it was withdrawn by British Railways and then sold for scrap to Woodham Bros, Barry. in the mid-1960s.

With Alderbottom Viaduct on the former Stubbins to Accrington Railway providing the backdrop, L&YR 0-6-0 Class 27 locomotive No. 52322 hauls a short goods train on 25 October 1995. The next stop is Irwell Vale station. The former L&YR locomotive was designed by John Aspinall and was built in 1896 at Horwich Works. It is the sole example of what was once a class of 484 locomotives.

It is not every day that you get opportunities like this! In amazing lighting conditions and in between rain showers, the sun lights up the scene, all with the added bonus of not one rainbow but two, albeit a faint one. L&Y Class 27 No. 52322 passes Burrs foot crossing with its short goods train on 25 October 1995.

A view showing the Lancashire countryside at its best during the early part of the autumn season, with Tor Hill and Musberry Heights forming the backdrop. L&Y Class 27 No. 52322 continues to haul its goods train to Irwell Vale station, which is located at the extreme right of this image. (25 October 1995)

In cold, crisp conditions, and after departing Irwell Vale station, BR 9f No. 92203 produces a nice trailing steam exhaust for the waiting gallery at Blackburn Road bridge (Ewood Bridge) as it hauls the 10.00 Bury to Rawtenstall train on 29 October 1995.

Not a combination you would have seen during the British Railway era, but a colourful combination nevertheless during a railway gala event. Being highlighted by the low autumn sun is Ivatt Class No. 46441 leading A4 Class No. 60007 *Sir Nigel Gresley* as they pass Burrs foot crossing with the 15.00 Bury to Rawtenstall train. The train was part of the line's autumn steam gala weekend. (29 October 1995)

Sometimes, when a previous day's weather produced a considerable amount of rain, the result was unexpected pools of water. One such location was near the River Irwell bridge at Fernhill where, at the top of the embankment, such a pool was created. This provided an unusual – perhaps one-off – opportunity to catch a reflection of a train crossing the bridge. By good fortune this was possible on 2 November 1995 when L&YR Class 27 No. 52322 was hauling another goods train for the benefit of a group of photographers.

The author makes no apologies for showing a number of train silhouette images in this book; the East Lancashire Railway had some of the best locations on any preserved line in the United Kingdom to achieve such images. In this instance, with the sun partly hidden by the clouds and steam exhaust, the outline of No. 52322 and goods train is shown to good effect as it approaches Touch Hill Cutting at Burrs on 2 November 1995.

In low autumn sun, L&YR Class 27 No. 52322 and goods train work across Brooksbottom Viaduct on the approach to Nuttall Tunnel. In the background, and built in 1876 by Edward Hoyle. Sadly, in 2016 the building partially collapsed into the river and was subsequently demolished. Fortunately, the main mill building remains and now houses private apartments. (2 November 1995)

A modern interpretation of a yesteryear image. The locomotive crew take on water for No. 52322 from a nearby water tower at Rawtenstall station. In the background still stands one of the tall chimneys and mill that were very common in this part of Lancashire as part of the cotton industry. Had this been taken in black and white you may have mistaken it as being from the 1950s instead. (25 October 1995)

Taken on Boxing Day in 1995 and entering what is known as the golden hour, when the sun appears to turn gold as it sets in the last hour of daylight. L&YR No. 52322 and a short three-coach train catches the rays of the setting sun as it crosses Brooksbottom Viaduct on the 15.00 train to Rawtenstall.

The sun has set beyond the houses in the background and now, in the twilight hour, the sky produces a glow to show the unmistakable outline of the L&YR Class 27 No. 52322 and its crew as it crosses the River Irwell bridge at Fernhill with the 16.00 train to Rawtenstall. (27 December 1995)

In golden sunlight Black Five No. 45337 makes a stirring sight as it passes Burrs foot crossing with the 15.00 four-coach train to Rawtenstall on 28 December 1995. No. 45337 was originally built by Armstrong Whitworth, Newcastle upon Tyne, for the LMS in 1937 and was in service until 1965 while based at Carlisle Kingmoor. In 1983, it was purchased from Woodham Bros, Barry, by 26B Railway Co. who eventually restored it to working order at Bury in early 1995.

Sunshine and snow always make a great combination, especially when it coincides with the Winter Steam Gala weekend at the railway. In this instance the author, attempting to take some cover from an easterly breeze in Touch Hill Cutting, Burrs, catches BR 9f No. 92203 *Black Prince* working the 12.30 Bury to Rawtenstall train on 28 January 1996.

During Steam Gala weekends the railway attempt to operate an intensive train service with added variety to cater for all enthusiasts' tastes. This includes operating goods train within the timetable. In this image, Black Five No. 45337 is passing Fernhill with the 13.35 goods train to Ramsbottom consisting of six box vans, three tanks, four open wagons as well as a brake van at either end of the train. (28 January 1996)

An unusual sight of little and large locomotives together. Here is the outline of L&YR 0-6-0 No. 52322 leading BR 9f No 92203 on the 16.00 Bury to Rawtenstall train as they head towards Touch Hill Cutting at Burrs on 28 January 1996 as part of the Steam Gala Weekend. Certainly, No. 92203 could easily push No. 52322 and haul its train with ease on its own, but it does nevertheless provide a spectacular sight.

While the setting sun peaks below the footplate of the locomotive, it creates an unmistakable silhouette of BR A4 No. 60007 *Sir Nigel Gresley* as she passes Burrs foot crossing on the 17.00 Bury to Rawtenstall train during the railway's Steam Gala event on 28 January 1996.

The author's wish comes true, finally seeing BR Coronation Class No. 46229 *Duchess of Hamilton* posed at Bury Bolton Street station. It is complete with a Merseyside Express headboard and also, importantly, the author's home shed – an 8A (Edge Hill) shed code with the permission of the National Railway Museum. During the early 1960s, the *Duchess* was based at Edge Hill and also likely appeared on the Merseyside Express train too while based there. As such, an opportunity was presented and taken, much to the pleasure of the author. (16 February 1996)

When the *Duke* met the *Duchess*! Two iconic locomotives together: No. 71000 *Duke of Gloucester* faces No. 46229 *Duchess of Hamilton* in Buckley Wells yard on 24 February 1996. Sadly, for the foreseeable future these two locomotives will unlikely meet again due to No. 46229 now being back in her LMS streamlined casing as No. 6229 and locked away at the National Railway Museum.

Resplendent in her BR lined maroon livery and still adoring her 8A shed code, No. 46229 *Duchess of Hamilton* passes Burrs foot crossing with the 14.00 Bury to Rawtenstall short four-coach train. Add in a few telegraph posts and this could almost be an image taken in the early 1960s, when No. 46229 and some of her sisters were seen hauling short trains in and around the North West of England. (10 March 1996)

Not long after sunrise on a cold, frosty morning on 27 December 1996, ex-GWR 2-8-0T No. 4277 departs Buckley Wells yard with an empty three-coach stock train and heads to Bury Bolton Street station to operate the first passenger train of the day. No. 4277 had arrived on loan from the North Yorkshire Moors Railway only a few weeks previously. (Courtesy of Brian Dobbs)

Working the first train of the new year and in excellent winter sunlight, 2-8-0T No. 4277 approaches Blackburn Road bridge (Ewood Bridge) with its four-coach train. The next stop is Rawtenstall station. (1 January 1997)

With the backdrop of Irwell Vale village among the surrounding snowy countryside and making a spirited departure from the station, 2-8-0T No. 4277 gets into her stride with the 12.15 Bury to Rawtenstall train on 1 January 1997. No. 4277 was built by the Great Western Railway at Swindon Works in 1920 and was used mainly on short-haul coal trains in the Welsh Valleys. It was withdrawn by British Railways in 1964 and sent to Woodham Bros, Barry.

Nothing can beat a steam train in the landscape, especially in splendid wintery, snowy, light conditions as portrayed in this image. No. 4277 – now bunker first – departs from Irwell Vale station with the return 11.00 Rawtenstall to Bury train. Beyond Irwell Vale village are the peaks of Tor Hill and Musberry Heights. (1 January 1997)

An interesting recreation of yesteryear took place among the setting of Castlecroft yard and the old goods warehouse on 20 May 1997. The driver of ex-L&YR 0-4-ST *Pug* No. 51218 is waiting for someone to turn up to load some barrels into a 12T box van, which are on a Sentinel Steam Wagon – built in 1932 in the livery of the Cardiff Gas Light & Coke Company. The *Pug* was built in 1901 by the Lancashire & Yorkshire Railway, withdrawn by British Railways in 1964 and purchased by the Lancashire & Yorkshire Railway Trust shortly afterwards. (Courtesy of Brian Dobbs)

In surreal, early morning lighting conditions the sun attempts to highlight the nine-coach train hauled by GWR 4-6-0 Castle Class No. 5029 *Nunney Castle* as she is reflected in a pool of frozen water near to Burrs foot crossing on 12 December 1997. Alas, on the day there was a small westerly wind that blew the locomotive's exhaust over and prevented the sun in lighting up some of the train, including No. 5029; nevertheless, it has still produced an unusual image.

Perhaps not an image for the purists. The original image was taken with a Hoya orange graduated lens filter in order to accentuate the glow of the setting sun in the background. This shows the classic outline of 4-6-2 Coronation Class No. 46229 *Duchess of Hamilton* as she passes Burrs with a private charter train for Ramsbottom station on 25 January 1998.

The power of the *Duchess*! An image and angle that shows off the majesty of No. 46229 *Duchess of Hamilton* as she makes light work of her six-coach private charter at Burrs foot crossing on 24 February 1998. By this time, with the permission of the National Railway Museum and on the condition that she was eventually repainted back into lined maroon livery, with donations from many photographers, No. 46229 was painted into British Railways lined Brunswick green livery as portrayed in the early 1950s.

With only four weeks left of her boiler ticket remaining and, unknown to the author at the time, the following two images were sadly the last occasion he would see No. 46229 *Duchess of Hamilton* live in steam and working a train. The first image shows the *Duchess* resplendent in her Brunswick green livery working across Brooksbottom Viaduct while the loco crew savour the experience. In the second image, looking down on Brooksbottom Viaduct with Summerseat in the background, the *Duchess* again works its six-coach train before heading into Nuttall Tunnel. (24 February 1998)

The right locomotive for the right line? BR Mogul No. 42765 and the railway were made for each other, especially being in the heart of former Lancashire and Yorkshire territory. In this view, and taking the opportunity to photograph from below the embankment, No. 42765 passes Burrs foot crossing with the 12.00 Bury to Rawtenstall seven-coach train on 22 February 1998.

When this image was taken the East Lancashire Railway had built up an excellent reputation with the National Railway Museum (NRM) at York. As a result, the NRM decided to use the railway for running in turns for former LNER 2-6-2 Class V2 locomotive No. 60800 *Green Arrow* after her completion of her restoration. Seen here on an early hazy morning, *Green Arrow* passes Burrs foot crossing with a six-coach private charter. (2 September 1998)

Crossing the River Irwell bridge at Fernhill, No. 60800 *Green Arrow* makes a stirring sight as she powers her six-coach charter train towards Burrs and Summerseat on 2 September 1998. No. 60800 was designed by Nigel Gresley for the London & North Eastern Railway, and was built in 1936 at Doncaster Works as No. 4771. She was the first of the class and named after an express freight service. She was withdrawn by British Railways in 1962 and selected for preservation within the national collection, being the sole survivor of a class of 184 locomotives.

Looking out of the cab window of BR V2 No. 60800 *Green Arrow* is Ray Towell, a well-respected railway engineer of the National Railway Museum who was overseeing the trials at the railway of the three-cylinder locomotive. Sadly, Ray Towell passed away some years later in 2016; he is missed by all who knew him. In this view, the locomotive departs Ramsbottom station with her six-coach train and is now heading to Irwell Vale on 2 September 1998.

Passing Lumb on the final approach to Irwell Vale station, BR V2 No. 60800 *Green Arrow* makes short work of her train. Her clean exhaust gives the impression she was running smoothly; however, although not apparent, all was not well with her boiler. After the trials were completed a number of repairs had to be carried out before she returned to action and working on the UK mainline. (2 September 1998)

For the benefit of the waiting photographers, No. 60800 *Green Arrow*, looking well in her British Railways lined Brunswick green livery, produces a spirited clean exhaust as she does a run past at Irwell Vale station with her six-coach train. Unfortunately, in time *Green Arrow* was eventually returned for static display back in the National Railway Museum where she returned to her original LNER apple green livery as No. 4771. (2 September 1998)

After the boiler certificate had expired on No. 46229 *Duchess of Hamilton*, and as part of the agreement with the National Railway Museum and prior to be putting back on display at York, it was repainted into British Railways lined maroon livery once again. Under the floodlights at Buckley Wells yard she is seen in showroom appearance, accompanied with No. 60800 *Green Arrow*. (2 September 1998)

Another locomotive that changed its appearance while at the railway was BR 2-6-0 Ivatt Class No. 46441, which had been in the owner's preferred colour of BR(M) maroon livery but was repainted into BR lined black livery and looking very much the part too. Framed by a tree, she is seen working past Burrs foot crossing with the 15.00 Bury to Rawtenstall train on Remembrance Sunday 1998 (8 November) – hence the wreath on the smokebox door.

Visiting from the Dean Forest Railway and appearing in BR plain black livery is ex-Great Western Railway 0-4-2T No. 1450 making a spirited departure from Irwell Vale station with the 09.30 Bury to Rawtenstall train on 28 November 1998. No. 1450 was designed by Charles Collett and built in 1936 at Swindon Works, mainly working auto trains on the Abingdon Branch before being withdrawn in 1965 and then purchased by the Dart Valley Railway. (Courtesy of Kevin Truby)

In glorious, crisp, winter morning sunlight, Black Five No. 45407 departs away from Ramsbottom station with the 10.00 Bury to Rawtenstall train on 10 January 1999 – now owned by Ian Riley and looking superb in her BR lined black livery. No. 45407 has been a stalwart of the UK mainline scene since the 1980s and continues to this day, which is no mean feat and says much about the two owners of the locomotive during that period too.

It is winter days like this that make the time and effort to obtain photographs like this worthwhile. Producing a smoke ring and a crisp exhaust, Black Five No. 45407 works away from Irwell Vale station with the 12.00 Bury to Rawtenstall train. (10 January 1999)

During the winter of 1999/2000, former LNER 4-6-2 Class A2 No. 60532 *Blue Peter* arrived at the railway in between mainline operations. It was primarily used during the January and February Gala Steam weekends. Although not in steam, she is seen at Bury Bolton Street station posing with a matching rake of maroon coaches for the benefit of the attending photographers at this specially arranged evening on 7 February 2000. (Courtesy of Brian Dobbs)

Diesels at the East Lancashire Railway

The East Lancashire Railway also operate diesel locomotives, which provide cover especially outside the peak period timetable service, as well as catering for the diesel enthusiast at specially arranged gala events. The next fifteen pages present a selection of ex-BR diesels that have operated on the line during the 1990s and hopefully give a flavour of these trains.

Arguably the railway's best-known diesel belongs to the Class Forty Preservation Society: No. 40145, seen here at Bury South signal box in her original British Railways green livery as No. D345. This represents how the locomotive first appeared when released from the Vulcan Foundry in 1961 and before she received her yellow front warning panel. No. D345 was purchased in February 1984 and eventually she was returned to full working order, including being certificated to work passenger trains on the UK mainline. Behind the Class 40, also in matching livery, is the railway's resident Class 08 shunter: No. 08164, formerly No. D3232. (2 September 1998)

Passing the old goods warehouse at Summerseat and former British Railways 0-6-0 diesel-hydraulic locomotive No. D9531 works a morning Rawtenstall to Bury train during a Diesel Gala weekend event on 4 October 1992. No. 9531 was built at Swindon Works in 1965 was eventually designated a Class 14 by British Railways and subsequently sold in 1968. The locomotive spent most of its life under National Coal Board ownership until the early 1980s. In 1987, it arrived at the railway and returned to working order until 1997 where it commenced a major overhaul.

An image that portrays an everyday British Rail scene from the 1980s, but it was actually taken on 28 November 1992 on the ELR. In blue and grey livery a two-car Class 110 diesel multiple unit (E51813 and E51842) approach Touch Hill Cutting, Burrs, with a mid-afternoon Rawtenstall to Bury train. The Class 110 DMU were known as 'Calder Valley' units and spent most of their lives working around the north of England until the late 1980s. The two-car set was purchased in 1990 and eventually received a centre car (E59701) in 1994.

The railway's Diesel Gala events always produced unusual locomotive combinations, and this image is no exception. Passing Touch Hill Cutting at Burrs, three locomotives form the mid-afternoon Bury to Rawtenstall train: former BR Class 24 No. D5054 in green livery and Class 25s No. 25262 in blue livery and No. D7569 in the 1960s British Railways two-tone green livery. (5 June 1993)

Taken on 5 June 1993, with Nuttall Park and Ramsbottom in the background, former British Railways diesel-hydraulic Warship Class No. D832 *Onslaught* approaches Nuttall Tunnel with the 14.45 Rawtenstall to Bury train during the Diesel Gala weekend. No. D832, portrayed here in early BR black livery, was built at Swindon Works in 1961 and withdrawn in late 1972. She eventually entered preservation in 1979 and is only one of two that survived out of a class of thirty-eight locomotives.

Diesel-hydraulic locomotives meet at Ramsbottom station on 5 June 1994 during the Diesel Gala Weekend. Ex-Class 14 *Teddy Bear* No. D9531 is waiting as ex-Class 52 Western locomotive No. D1041 *Western Prince* approaches with the 15.00 Bury to Rawtenstall train. *Western Prince* was built at BR Crewe Works in 1962 and had a working life of just over fourteen years, mainly working passenger trains between London and the West Country before being withdrawn in 1976.

Owned by Pete Waterman, ex-BR Class 46 *Peak* No. 46035, seen here in her former British Railways green livery as No. D172 and now named *Ixion*, approaches Burrs foot crossing with the 14.00 Rawtenstall to Bury train during the Diesel Gala event on 5 June 1994. The Class 46 became the first preserved diesel to work on the UK mainline in October 1995 after being withdrawn by British Rail in 1990.

With owner Pete Waterman at the controls of Class 20 No. 20042, and paired with classmate No. 20188, they approach Fernhill with the 10.00 Bury to Rawtenstall train during the Diesel Gala event on 15 June 1995. Both locomotives (which were mainlined certificated) are in the black livery of the London North Western Railway, which was owned by Pete Waterman. (Courtesy of Kevin Truby)

Entering Touch Hill Cutting at Burrs, Brush Class 47 No. 47402 (D1501) *Gateshead* leads English Electric Class 40 No. 40145 on the 14.00 Rawtenstall to Bury train. This image was taken on 17 June 1995 during the railway's Diesel Gala event where both locomotives were resident at the railway and remained in their former British Rail plain blue livery of the late 1960s and 1970s. (Courtesy of Kevin Truby)

An impressive line of traction at Buckley Wells shed yard on the evening of 25 June 1995. From front to back: Class 20 No. 20042 in black LNWR livery, Class 47 No. D1842 in two-tone green BR livery, Peaks Class 46 No. D172 and Class 45 No. D120 both in BR early 1960s green livery, with a Class 121 (Bubble Car) and a two-car Class 117 Diesel Multiple Unit at the rear.

In all over BR plain blue livery, Class 50 No. 50015 *Valiant* with its six coaches approaches Irwell Vale station with the 11.30 Rawtenstall to Bury train on 6 June 1996. The Class 50 was built by English Electric at the Vulcan Works, Newton-le-Willows, in 1968. It was withdrawn by British Rail in 1992 and is now owned by the Bury Valiant Group. (Courtesy of Kevin Truby)

Looking splendid in ex-Finsbury Park BR blue livery, Class 55 (Deltic) No. 55015 *Tulyar* works the 09.50 Rawtenstall to Bury train as it approaches the next stop at Irwell Vale station on 8 March 1997. No. 55015 was a product of English Electric and part of a class of twenty-two locomotives that spent most of their lives hauling passenger trains on the East Coast mainline up to 1980. (Courtesy of Kevin Truby)

Visiting from the National Railway Museum is another Class 55 (Deltic) locomotive. No. 55002 *The Kings Own Yorkshire Light Infantry* is seen working away from Irwell Vale station and approaching Lumb with the 10.40 Rawtenstall to Bury train on 8 March 1997. The livery on No. 55002 was in its withdrawn condition by British Rail on 2 January 1981. The twenty-two-strong class of locomotives were either named after army regiments or famous racehorses and were all built at the Vulcan Foundry in Newton-le-Willows during 1961. (Courtesy of Kevin Truby)

The author makes no apologies for presenting another image of Class 55 No. 55002 *The Kings Own Yorkshire Light Infantry*, this time carrying a BR Eastern Deltic 20th anniversary headboard. In the nice afternoon sun, No. 55002 passes Horncliffe foot crossing with the 15.40 Rawtenstall to Bury train on 8 March 1997. In the background you are able to make out Townsend Fold signal box and crossing. (Courtesy of Kevin Truby)

Credit must be given to the many volunteers of the East Lancashire Railway who have restored this Class 110 Diesel 1960s Multiple Unit back to its original as-built condition of the early 1960s. Seen here on the approach to Summerseat station are car numbers DM Brake Composite 51813, Trailer Second 59701 and DM Composite 51842 with the 09.42 Bury to Rawtenstall train on 5 July 1997. This is the only surviving three-car Class 110 in existence, although there is a two-car version surviving at the Lakeside and Haverthwaite Railway. (Courtesy of Kevin Truby)

Passing Lumb on the approach to Irwell Vale station, now in two-tone green livery, No. D7612 ex-BR Class 25 No. 25262 works the 10.00 Bury to Rawtenstall train on 7 July 1997 during the railway's Diesel Gala event. No. D7612 was built in 1966 at BR Derby Works as part of a class of 327 locomotives. It was eventually withdrawn by British Rail in March 1987 as No. 25901 but was purchased in September 1989 and arrived at the East Lancashire Railway in the same month. (Courtesy of Kevin Truby)

Visiting from the National Railway Museum, Brush Type 2 A1A-A1A No. D5500, in her original British Railways green livery, is seen approaching Blackburn Road bridge with the 10.00 Bury to Rawtenstall train on 8 July 1997. No. D5500 was the first locomotive built by Brush under the 1955 BR modernisation plan in 1957. She eventually became No. 31018 under the TOPS numbering system (Class 31) and was withdrawn in 1976, being claimed by the Science Museum for preservation due to her historical significance. (Courtesy of Kevin Truby)

Just after crossing the River Irwell ex-Class 33 No. 33117 approaches the Little Cutting at Fernhill with the 15.00 Rawtenstall to Bury train on 8 July 1997 during the Diesel Gala event. No. 33117 was built by the Birmingham Railway Carriage & Wagon Company in 1960 as No. D6536. It operated on the Southern Region before being withdrawn in 1993, then was secured for preservation by the ELR. (Courtesy of Kevin Truby)

What is the author's favourite class of diesel locomotive? Approaching the Drum Works near to Fernhill, English Electric Type 4 locomotive No. D335 is on the 10.00 Rawtenstall to Bury train during the Diesel Gala Traction Day on 9 July 1997. No. D335 was built in 1960 at the Vulcan Works, Newton-le-Willows, and eventually renumbered '40135' under the TOPS scheme in 1973. She continued to operate until December 1986 (by then as No. 97406) when she was finally withdrawn and then purchased by the Class 40 Preservation Society in 1988. (Courtesy of Kevin Truby)

An amazing sight – and sound – at Burrs foot crossing. With 6,000 hp at the head of the train, there is no doubt of the popularity of the 17.00 Bury to Rawtenstall train by the number of enthusiasts with their heads sticking out of coach windows! Well, with three matching livery Class 40s at the front you cannot go far wrong! No. D335 (40135) is leading Nos D200 (40122) and D345 (40145), providing the entertainment on 9 July 1997. (Courtesy of Kevin Truby)

An interesting image showing the single line token being passed from the signalman to the driver of BR Class 27 No. 27001 on departure from Ramsbottom station with the 11.20 Bury to Rawtenstall train on 4 July 1998. No. 27001, owned by the Scottish Railway Preservation Group, who purchased the locomotive for preservation in the late 1980s, was on a quick visit to the railway from the Bo'ness Railway to participate in the line's Diesel Gala event. (Courtesy of Fred Kerr)

There is no doubt as to the time of year with heavy green summer foliage in view. Ex-BR Class 45 No. 45060 *Sherwood Forester* approaches Irwell Vale station with the 11.20 Bury to Rawtenstall train. In the background you are able to make out the outline of Alderbottom Viaduct on the former Stubbins to Accrington line. Class 45 (Peak) No. 45060 was built in 1961 at BR Derby Works as No. D100 and withdrawn in December 1985 before being preserved for further use. (Courtesy of Kevin Truby)

With the visit of Class 35 Hymek No. D7017 from the West Somerset Railway, the opportunity was taken to double-head with the railway's own Hymek, No. D7076, during the Summer Diesel Gala weekend. On an overcast day, No. D7076 leads No. D7017 as they are about to depart Irwell Vale station with the 13.00 Bury to Rawtenstall train on 8 July 1998. Both locomotives were originally built in 1962 by Beyer Peacock, Manchester, and were subsequently withdrawn in the early 1970s. (Courtesy of Fred Kerr)

Taken at the top of the head shunt of Castlecroft Goods Yard on 2 September 1998, is an image of the sole survivor of a Metropolitan Vickers Co-Bo class of locomotives – No. D5705. This locomotive was built in 1958 and later designated as a Class 28 before being withdrawn by British Rail in 1975. She only survived due to being used by the BR Research Division, along with being a Carriage Heating Unit before being purchased for preservation and arriving at Matlock in 1980. Currently, No. D5705 is being restored back to full working order, although this is a long-term project.

Passing the home signal for Ramsbottom station, BR Class 44 No. 44004 *Great Gable* slows down for the road crossing with the 10.15 Rawtenstall to Bury train on 4 July 1999. Originally built in 1959 at BR Derby Works as No. D4, she was part of a class of ten locomotives that were all named after British Mountains – hence the reason for the class being given the nickname 'Peaks', along with the subsequent Class 45 and 46s. No. 44004 was withdrawn in 1980 and purchased by the Peak Locomotive Company, based at the Midland Railway, Butterley. (Courtesy of Fred Kerr)

Another English Electric product of Vulcan Works, and in lined Brunswick Green livery, BR Class 50 No. 50007 *Sir Edward Edgar* departs from Irwell Vale station with the 13.15 Rawtenstall to Bury train on 11 July 1999. Later in her life No. 50007 was unique among the fifty-strong class as she was repainted into her present livery and named *Sir Edward Elgar* in connection with the 150th anniversary of the Great Western Railway in 1984, unlike the remainder of the class, which retained their Royal Navy ship names. (Courtesy of Fred Kerr)

Although withdrawn at the time of this image, Class 47 No. 47306 *The Sapper* was visiting the railway courtesy of the English, Scottish & Welsh Railway, being part of their Heritage Fleet. It is seen here looking attractive in her Railfreight Distribution livery and passing Summerseat station with the 09.35 Rawtenstall to Bury train on 10 September 1999. (Courtesy of Fred Kerr)

Passing Class 33 No. 33117 in the shunt siding, ex-BR Class 56 No. 56006 is showing off her gleaming plain blue paintwork as she approaches Ramsbottom station with the 11.15 Rawtenstall to Bury train on 10 September 1999 during the EWS Classic Traction Event. The locomotive became part of the EWS Heritage Locomotive fleet and subsequently visited other events before she was officially withdrawn in December 2003. (Courtesy of Fred Kerr)

Looking splendid in its BR Civil Engineers (Dutch) livery, No. 33202 *The Burma Star* approaches Rawtenstall station with the ex-12.55 Bury train during the EWS Classic Heritage event on 10 September 1999. No. 33202 was built at BR Crewe Works in 1962 as No. D6587. It was withdrawn in December 1998 and subsequently preserved, as well as having another – albeit short – period back on the UK mainline. (Courtesy of Fred Kerr)

Unusual visitors to the line, and part of the EWS Classic Heritage event were Class 73s No. 73133 *Bluebell Railway* in mainline blue livery and No. 73129 *City of Winchester* in Network South East livery, seen arriving at Rawtenstall station with the ex-13.45 Bury train on 10 September 1999. Both locomotives were built by English Electric at their Vulcan Foundry in the mid-1960s and have the ability to draw their power either from Direct Current Third Rail or from its in-built diesel engine. (Courtesy of Fred Kerr)

Another feast of English Electric power: the drivers open up the throttle on three Class 37 locomotives, much to the delight of the onboard enthusiasts as they pass Burrs foot crossing. Leading is No. 37906 *Star of the East* in Transrail grey livery, with No. 37029 in BR plain blue livery and No. 37002 in Transrail Dutch livery on the 17.10 Bury to Rawtenstall train on 12 September 1999. (Courtesy of Fred Kerr)